# My Grandfather is a Cowboy

Poems by

## Sharon Waller Knutson

In memory of my beloved grandfather, William Charles Marvin (1882-1957) and father, Waldo Emerson Waller. (1907-1989)

# Acknowledgments

I thank the following publications for publishing my poems:

*Autumn Sky Poetry:* "Mothers of Lost Children"

*Impspired:* "Splashing into Sunlight."

*Lothlorien*: "Arizona Monsoon," "Ballad of Big Bad Bob," "Crow's Feet," "Octogenarian Cowboy," "Toddler Houdini," "Frankie and Dave," Some Have It, Some Don't" and "The Chicken Dance."

*ONE ART:* "Connections" and "On the Second Anniversary of His Death."

*My Grandmother Smokes Chesterfields (Flutter Press)* "At the Rodeo" and "Driving the Cows to Market."

*Poetry Breakfast:* "Care Loving."

*Red Eft Review*: "Bailing Our Grandson Out of Jail," "Counterfeit Cowboy, "Gunshots Ring Out" and "Staying Alive.

*Rye Whiskey Review*: "Do you Ever Think of Me?" "Easter Egg Hunt" and "The Bloody Mary Moon."

*Silver Birch Press (Spice and Seasoning Series:)* "My Father's Pickle Factory."

*Spillwords:* "Hide Black Cats on Halloween, the Vets Warn" as "On Halloween."

*Storyteller Poetry Review*: "Turkey Day Cooking Lessons."

*The Beatnik Cowboy*: "Cyber Urban Cowboy," "I'm the Wife, She Says" and "Our Grandchildren's Other Grandfather."

*Verse Virtual:* "Canine Rock Band," "Heir to the Throne," "My Father is Color Blind," "Nature's Designer Cat," "Surprise, My Husband Says," "Standoff at Elephant Butte," "Tanya Tucker Wannabe," "The Naughty Hen" and "What Do I Do With My Body When I Die."

# Contents

# Growing Up in Montana

# My Grandfather is a Cowboy

As a child, with soft fingers
I trace his hands, calloused
from roping cattle, his boots
and belt buckle, worn out
from breaking wild horses.
By the time I am born,
he has a bum leg and doesn't
do much riding or roping.

He bans my sister, my cousins
and me from the ranch where he
feeds and waters the rodeo stock
fearing we'll feed them apples
and the brahmas and broncs
won't buck at the rodeo.

He also fears we'll be bit
by a pit viper with a diamond
shaped head and be forced
to suck and spit out the venom
on our skin to save our young lives.

When I am sixteen and learning
to drive, Uncle Jack takes
me out to the ranch and I never go back.
I'll never forget the outhouse.
I couldn't get the stink of urine
and feces out of my nostrils
or the sight out of my head

of the naked people
in the dirty magazines.

Your grandfather is tough
*as leather,* my mother says.
When she was a child,
he quit whiskey cold turkey,
by gathering his children
around. They hugged him as he
shook and sweat. *Never drank
another drop since,* she swears.

I silently wish he'd teach
that trick to my cowboy father
who hides beer and whiskey bottles
all over the house and yard
and staggers to climb in the saddle
to pick up bucked off cowboys
at my grandfather's rodeo grounds.

# The Cowboy and the Lady

My father blows into town
with the Montana wind.
Hops off the freight train
hauling Idaho spuds,

swigs whiskey, tosses
the empty bottle,
follows the railroad
tracks to Will's Café,

where he sees my mother
in a white waitress uniform,
bouffant red hair, hanging
a Help Wanted Sign.

She smells his breath when
he removes his cowboy hat
and introduces himself
as her new chef. She warns

my grandfather not to hire him.
*He's trouble.* As his cook walks out
just as the customers walk in,
my grandfather hands my father

the chef's whites and ushers him
to the kitchen and soon the café
is filled with the aroma of sizzling
bacon, burgers and onion rings.

I imagine how my mother melts
like the butter in the pan and the ice
cream in the cones when my father's
hand brushes hers as he slides

the hot plates towards her, when he
opens the door, hands her the menu,
and she gets swept up in his laughter
and his eyes as dark and deep

as the muddy river as she falls
in love, not even noticing
the jagged rocks, rapids
and undertow pulling her under.

# My Father is Color Blind

I am four and riding my Shetland Pony,
Sissy, and my father is riding Zephr,
his Arabian, who leads the July 4th
parade every year and races fast
around the barrels and chasing
the calves my father hog ties
in record time at the rodeo.
Today Zephr plods along the road.

Where do you want to ride today?
my father asks, unusually jovial.
*Past the blue house,* I say.
Instead, he leads us past
the green house with the Bay
and Palomino in the pasture.

Both run to the fence and neigh
and Sissy scared and startled
by the sight of strange horses
bucks like a bronc in the rodeo,
tossing me in the air and I land
on the road on my left side.

My father orders me to get up
but I can't. Hot pain shoots
through my arm and leg.
I hear tires squeal, a car door
slam and my mother shouting,
*You're drunk. What did you do?*

*She's fine, Just get up,* he says.
Then I hear Aunt Babs voice,
of reason. *Don't move her.*
*Her arm and leg look broken.*

Mother rides with me in the ambulance
and stays with me as I lay in a hospital
bed for what seems like forever
with my left leg in traction and my left arm
in a plaster cast which my grandparents,
aunts, uncles, cousins and neighborhood
kids all sign, as they crowd in the room.
The only person missing is my father.

*He's away on a trip*, my mother
says. *He's on a bender, the coward,*
my grandmother mumbles.
*He can't face what he did.* I worry
about my father. *It wasn't his fault,*
I say. *He's color blind.*

I never sit in a saddle again.
I wish I could say it scares
my father sober but it doesn't.
He drinks booze until at 65
a judge says: *Get Sober*
*or go to jail.* He never drinks again.

# Easter Egg Hunt

All dressed up
in bonnets,
crinoline,
and patten leather
at two and five
my sister and I find
hidden
in the back yard
a dozen colored
eggs and two
bottles
which mama
snatches
out of our baskets
and pours
the stinking liquid
that smells
like daddy
down the drain.

# The Bloody Mary Moon

is lighting up our yard
and my memories.
I can see my grandmother
in her curlers and housecoat
pouring V-8 Juice, Vodka,
and Worcestershire Sauce
into a mason jar and stirring
in salt and pepper before drinking
it down as I eat my Cheerios
with milk and drink my orange
juice in my pajamas. When I ask
what she is drinking and if I can
have some, she says, *Bloody Mary.*
*Only for adults.* One time I take
a sip when she turns her back
and it tastes so nasty
I decide to be a child forever.

# Turkey Day Cooking Lessons

*It is wise to rub sage*
*on a turkey before roasting*
*it in a preheated oven,*
my teacher-chef father lectures.\

as he uses his finger to spread
the dried spice on the skin of a wild
turkey and sticks a MacIntosh
from our tree in the cavity.

*Bake your dressing outside the turkey,*
our mother says as she boils
giblets, celery, onions and broth,
pours over dry bread and bakes.

*Always make your own cranberry*
*sauce*, my mother says as she boils
fresh berries with water and sugar
as snow falls in Montana in the 1940s.

*Pies taste better when made from scratch,*
my grandmother says as she rolls
the dough and my sister and I cook
the pumpkin and add cinnamon and cloves.

I learn my lessons well and seven
decades later, I forgo the savory sage
mixes, Stovetop stuffing, canned
cranberry sauce and storebought pies

and rub my turkey with dried sage,
stuff it with an apple and make my
dressing, pie and cranberry sauce
from scratch as the sun shines in Arizona.

# Friday is Fish Night

We were not Catholic or religious
but every Friday for supper
my mother would fry trout
my grandfather, uncles or father
fished out of the Stillwater River.

In Billings, Butte and Yakima
my friends and I would gather
at the All You Could Eat Fish Fry
where we would chow down
on battered cod, chips and coleslaw.

At Fisherman's Wharf
and the Seattle Water Front
on Friday's we'd dine on fresh
crab, shrimp and sushi
with a salad or clam chowder.

Every Friday my mother-in-law
would flour and pan fry fresh
bass, bluegill, perch or trout
my father-in-law caught
in the fishing holes of Southeast Idaho.

It's Friday, my husband says,
in our home in the Arizona desert
as he fishes from the freezer
Wal-Mart salmon, Swai or tilapia
and pops it in the microwave.

# Saturday Nights

At the picture show,
we'd plunk down
two dimes to get in
and a nickel for a bag
of popcorn and another
nickel for a cup
of Coca-Cola over ice
and slide into our seats
on the front row
and squint at the screen
as Roy Rogers rode Trigger
with Bullet barking
as be shot outlaws.

When we got home,
we'd shed our clothes,
toss them in the hamper
for the Monday wash day
and slip into the bathtub,
soaping our hair with Prell
shampoo and bodies with bars
of Lifebouy soap, washing away
the dirt and grime of the week.

# Toilet Papering the Principal's House in the Fifties

Masked strangers toss
multiple rolls of toilet paper
up into the black sky
and it unrolls like ribbons
and wraps around the house

of the principal and his wife
Dressed as Ike and Mamie
as they stand next to me
disguised as Lois Lane
with Clark Kent at my side

as we serve Hawaiian punch
at the high school Halloween
party in the gymnasium.
The babysitter and neighbors
spot under the streetlight

the muscular Robin Hood,
lanky Lone Ranger, burlesque
bumblebee and plump pumpkin
before they vanish
like aliens in a spaceship.

Some of us speculate
the culprits are students
who had felt the principal's

paddle on their backside
but no one snitches.

The whole school suffers
the consequences as it takes
time to untangle the toilet
paper and return it to bathroom
stalls where it had been stolen.

# My Father's Favorite Word

*Marvelous,* my father murmurs
when my mother, whose name is Marvel,
walks into the room, high heels tapping,
green muumuu swishing, jewelry jangling
red hair ratted into a beehive,
and sets a skillet on the stove.

*Marvelous,* he sighs when he grills
the steak medium rare serves
it with baked potatoes with just enough
butter and salt to please the palate
tender vegetables and crisp salad
at the restaurants where he cooks.

But *marvelous* is not the word
he uses when he orders
Sirloin steak medium rare
and the waiter brings him
a plate of beef so rare
it is lying in a pool of blood
bellowing like a dying bull,
raw broccoli and wilted lettuce.

*Marvelous,* he says, when he picks
out the perfect dress for his blue eyed
blonde granddaughter whom he dotes
on like he does my sister and me when
we were young, as he shops
for dolls and dresses for Christmas.

*Marvelous,* he says when he sees
photos of his grandson, a mirror
image of himself. But he doesn't
live long enough to see his grandson
following in his footsteps,
teaching English, writing fiction
and grilling steaks to perfection
for his wife and two sons.

*Marvelous,* I say as I write poems
about my childhood and imagine
my father who would be 115
echoing my words no matter
whether he is teaching angels
or the devil to say *Marvelous*
when he grills their steak to perfection.

# My Grandfather's Rodeo Grounds

is a family affair in the summer
on the weekends. Standing on stout legs,
suspenders holding his pants up,
my grandfather, thinning gray
hair slick and parted, bellies up to the bar
and sells Schlitz and Coors on ice
to thirsty cowboys and patrons

while my sister and I sell orange soda
and root beer to kids from school.
My grandmother and my mother
and her sisters fry hamburgers
and roast hot dogs and slap
them on buns and sell them to folks
hungry for food and excitement.

My father's voice booms
on the loud speaker
like an auctioneer
as he announces the names
of the cowboys and cowgirls
who mount the bucking
broncs and brahmas, rope
the calves or race around
the barrels on quarter horses
and the winners of each event.

Uncle Bill and Jack take money
at the gate and my grandfather

pays the winning cowboys
and my father books hotel rooms
for wives and children of cowboys
hospitalized with broken bones.
During the week, my sister and I
run under the empty bleachers
picking up cans and coins
and sell them for spending money.

# At the Rodeo

The green chiffon scarf
ropes her long red curls.

But there is nothing to corral
my mother when the bull's horns

lift my father from his saddle
when he tries to rescue a fallen cowboy

and sends him flying like a rag doll
and when he lands the bull charges.

All she can see is the dust in the air
swirling above the shouting crowd.

My mother races down the bleacher steps
in her green dress and high heel pumps,

Not even noticing her scarf has slipped
and her curls have escaped into the wind.

She arrives at the fence in time to see
my father limping over to his horse Zephyr

whose white coat is tinged pink
where the bulls horns had branded him

realizing the horse has stepped
between my father and the bull,

As he has gotten between
my father and her for a decade,

my mother whips the scarf
off her neck and lassoes her curls

as my father flashes her a grin
and walks Zephyr out of the arena

as the crowd cheers and the ambulance
waits for the next cowboy to fall.

# The Big Red Barn

My father lifts heavy
bales of hay stored
in the big red barn to feed
Zephyr, his Arabian, Sissy,
my Shetland pony and Francis,
his friend, Buss's mule.

The barn sits behind the house
daddy rents for twenty dollars
a month on a residential
street in a small Montana town
in the nineteen forties and fifties.

By the time I am a teenager
and all the animals are gone
at 2 am one Sunday morning
we wake up to orange flames
shooting against a charcoal sky,
sirens screaming, voices
shouting, smoke billowing
and watch the old barn burn.

Firemen find Marlboro butts
and declare the fire arson.
My mother blames the couple
next door leaning on the fence
laughing, smoking and chugging
Coors like they are watching
a fireworks display on July 4th.

But my money is on Ricky
and Johnny who brag in school
how they bash the brains
of cats with baseball bats
in the barn as we sleep
while they suck on Marlboros
and blow smoke in our faces.

# My Grandfather's Saloon

Businessmen from Billings,
landowners from Laurel
and farmers from Park City
drive the old highway
on weekends to join the locals
at Will's Saloon, smack dab
in the middle of wheat farms
and cattle ranches in the 1950s.

Under neon lights, they sit
on swivel chairs at the bar
swilling Schlitz from the tap,
Jim Beam over ice, and Coors
from the can, as they snack
on pickled pigs' feet, pistachios
and peanuts, while a blonde
beauty in black bra and panties
blows them a kiss from the pinup
calendar on the wall.

Donning skirts, shorts. shirts
and Levi's, they drop a dime
in the jukebox to hear Tammy
and George singing *Golden Rings*
as they waltz and jitterbug in boots
and stilettos on the hardwood
floor of the old one room
school house my grandfather
turns into a western dance hall.

While the moon smiles in a black
sky, my seventy something
grandparents close the bar
and lock the dance hall
and retire to their apartment
behind the bar and soak
their tired bodies in a Claw Foot tub
filled with hot water and Epson salts
and fall asleep in their poster bed.

# Driving the Cows to Market

High on our cushioned thrones,
my grandfather and I sit.
He peers down at the black asphalt,
eyes milky with cataracts

and presses his one good foot
on the clutch, while I step
on the brake and shift gears.
Belching black smoke, the truck

lurches through town as the cargo
scrunched together and bawling
stare through the slats at the people
turning their heads and laughing.

I love the way his gnarled hands
feel on my shoulder as I guide
him through the crowd
and help him count the cash.

It is even worth it when the bullies
plug their noses when they pass me
in the hall or hose me down
when I walk past their picket fences.

But when I cannot awaken him
one market run, I want to grab
the matches sitting on the wood stove
and pour the kerosene from the lamps

and watch the smoke and flames rise
as the town burns like firewood.
Then I remember my grandfather's story
about the farmer who put blinders

on both sides of his horse's head
when it pulled the milk wagon so
It would ignore the distractions
and keep its eyes on the road.

After they cover him with the sheet
and take him away in his overalls,
I load the truck, climb into the driver's
seat and drive the cows to market.

# Uncle Worship

My mother's brothers
and brothers-in-law
were my teachers
and preachers.

Uncle Jack taught me
to drive a car
in-between his divorce
and dalliances.

Uncle Bill and Uncle Frank,
carpenters like Jacob,
taught me by example
marriage is forever.

My other Uncle Bill,
a policeman, taught me
the law works when he caught
my grandmother's swindler.

Uncle Emil, the train
conductor, with a red
nose of a circus clown,
taught me to laugh.

But it was Uncle Roger,
the frugal businessman
and Rock Hudson lookalike,
who taught me the most

when he rode his bicycle
as he did every morning
across a busy street
and a car wrecked our world.

# My Father's Pickle Factory

After my Grandpa Mack dies
in the late fifties, his century
old grocery store on the old
highway a mile out of town
shuts down. But farmers
he barters with for groceries
still have their debt to pay
so we always have fresh eggs
and milk, corn on the cob,
tomatoes and zucchini.

But one day shortly after
we arrive in the summer
a farmer backs his truck up
to the empty store
and unloads a pile of cucumbers
that fills a storeroom.

My grandmother's girdle
almost comes unzipped
but a lightbulb goes off in the brain
of my father/school teacher/chef.

*We'll make pickles,* he says.
He drives off to town and comes back
with two oak barrels, bags of pickling
salt and spice, a box full of farm fresh dill,
and a carton filled with bottles of vinegar.

My mother, sister and I toss
the cucumbers in the barrels
while my father gets out the hose
and fills the barrels with water, vinegar,
dill, pickling salt and spice, seals it up
and we wait until fall for the cucumbers
to ferment and preserve into pickles.

When we bite into the spears -,
flavorful, juicy and crisp - they crunch
in our mouths like the autumn leaves
under our shoes and tires. We eat dill
pickles for years out of the barrel
in the back of my Grandpa's store.

# Riding the Mail Truck on Christmas Eve in Montana

The mailman's moustache is white
as the snow that covers the hillsides
and rooftops of farmhouses and barns
as my sister and I bundled up in scarves,
stocking caps, mittens and wool coats
in below zero temperatures sit on mailsacks,
presents in our laps, and the mail truck
treks through a blizzard on back roads
from Billings to Broadus for 167 miles

It is the sixties and we are in our twenties
and my father will do anything to have
his daughters home for Christmas
even if it means enlisting the help
of the Postmaster. We run into a wall
of snow blocking the road at midnight
when like a shining star we see headlights

and a snowplow chipping at the wall
and we follow the taillights as it carves
a path for three miles and lead us
to the door of a two-story farmhouse
where my father and mother stand
in their bathrobes. anxiously awaiting.
the arrival of their only children.

My father waves to the mailman
and the snowplow driver, the father

of a student in the one-room schoolhouse
where he teaches Grades 1 to 12.
The mail truck picks us up Christmas
night and we ride back to Billings
following the snowplow as snow
continues to fall and pile up.

Neither rain nor sleet nor snow
can stop the mailman or the Waller
sisters from their appointed duties.

# Salt and Pepper

Growing up in Montana,
I wanted to be pure and serene
as the stray white cat we named Salt
and as feisty and fearless
as the black and white fox terrier
we named Pepper who took on dogs
twice his size. We always
managed to break up the fights
and save Pepper.  But this time
no one can pry the jaws of death
of Smokey my cousin's black and white
shepherd from Pepper's neck. We use
a rake and body power and finally spray
water from the hose, and still
Smokey won't let go until Salt
slips through the open screen door
and hops on Smokey's back, digging
her claws like spurs and rides
him like a bucking bronc up the street.
The entire neighborhood is cheering
and clapping like they are at the rodeo.
When Salt, satisfied she'd saved the day,
bails off the back of the yowling Smokey,
Pepper chases her into the house
and side by side they sit at the dinner table
begging for scraps as we sprinkle salt
and pepper on our meat and potatoes
and I wonder if we should rename
our pets Ginger and Nutmeg.

# The Naughty Hen

*That hen is the best layer in the house,*
his father tells my husband when he
is four and points to the big fat
brown hen as they gather eggs.

The child hears: *biggest liar*
and interprets his father to mean
it is his job as the firstborn to teach
the naughty chicken a lesson.

After supper, he sneaks out and snatches
the hen, takes her to the chopping block
and grabs the ax and chops off her head
just like he watched his father do.

He is so proud of his handiwork
that as soon as the deed is done,
he takes his parents outside and points
to the headless corpse and bloody

head with dead eyes wide open
thinking he will get hugs and ice cream
for a bedtime snack and is shocked
by the silence and then the shouting.

*Do you know what you've done?*
his father yells in his face.
*Of course, he doesn't,* his mother says.
*You let him watch you butcher chickens.*

His mother is quiet as she plucks
the feathers and boils the hen
for hours and then makes dumplings
and gravy and glares when he says mmmm.

He's not sure why he is being banned
from the hen house but he's happy
because he doesn't like to be pecked
on his hands when he hunts for eggs.

# Looney the Holstein

Big and black and white
with eyes brown as butter
burning in the skillet, Looney
earned her name when she
jumped the high fence
when placed in the milking
station and flew across
the pasture like a liberated
lady of the sixties resisting
restraints and rules.

She kicked like the Karate Kid
when at sixteen my husband
milked her every afternoon
after school and dodged
her hooves  heavy and hard
as she aimed for the groin or gut.

The last time he saw Looney,
he remembers her leg raising
for one last kick but he was ready
and he ducked and bobbed
as he pumped her teats
and warm and white milk
flowed into the bucket at his feet.

# Love In the West and Southwest

# Smoke and Mirrors

When I see him standing
underneath the Conoco
lights, his long lanky legs
leaning against the brick building,
smoking a Camel, dark curls
cascading from his cowboy hat,

I am a filly flirting with a stallion
but when he grinds the butt
of his cigarette with the heel
of his leather boots, I am a calf
hopelessly roped and hogtied.

His lips taste like tobacco
and his shirt smells like smoke.
I am nineteen and he is twenty-
five and I liked riding the country
roads in his pickup truck
on the weekends, checking
the mirror on the visor
for lipstick on my teeth.

I don't remember us ever
going to a movie or a restaurant.
Once he drives me to the college
dorm on a Sunday afternoon
and I go to introduce
him to my roommates and forget
his name. He never calls after that.

I still don't remember his name
but my sister does. She googles
him and finds an eighty-six-year
old man with the same name
in the same small town
I left when I was still a filly
and he a strong stallion.

# Gorgeous George

The softball cracks against the bat
and soars out of the park
as my boyfriend blows me
a kiss as he runs the bases.

We stand and cheer and clap,
my sister and I in baseball caps,
my mother in green scarf
and father in cowboy hat.

We sit in the bleachers in Yakima
where they spend the summer
with us in our house with hardwood
floors on the main drag.

They approve because he plays
their favorite sport, but I am mesmerized
because he has my father's dark eyes
and hair, and he makes me laugh.

Afterwards, we celebrate at Papa's
Pizza Place where we eat pepperoni
and cheese on flat crusts and drink
root beer in glass mugs. At the end

of summer and baseball, my parents
return to Montana and George
goes back to his high school sweetheart
who spent the summer in Sicily.

# Counterfeit Cowboy

He wore a black ten-gallon hat
and snakeskin boots and Levi's
so tight they painted his legs blue.

I never saw a gun but in Texas
he said, he wore a Saturday
night special in a holster on his hip.

*All of my friends did*, he said.
Murderers got six years
and victims got death.

He said he went to high school
in Lubbock with Waylon
Jennings and drove George

Jones home from the bars
when he was too drunk
to drive himself.  But he said

a lot of things like *I do*
and *Till Death do us Part*
with a mistress on the side

sexy as a sirloin sandwich
on rye with sweet pickles
mayo and mustard.

After his wedding to Wife No. 3
days before our divorce was final,
I figured everything was a lie,

until I found the photo album
with pictures of him drinking
whisky with Waylon and George.

# Broken Hearts Club

Tawny mane like a lion,
Leo told me he and his live-in
Lady Godiva used to ride
their pet elephant Ziggy
on Saturdays through
the streets of Escondido.

After she married a man
who looked just like him
and sent him photos
of carbon copy children
he sold Ziggy and spent
his weekends at *We Care*,

a support group for those
of us with broken hearts.
He taught me to laugh again
while we bowled strikes,
snuggled in a sleeping bag
on a Mexican beach, watched
Bergman movies in San Diego.
He wept with me, weaned
me off of sugar and valium.

But when my broken heart
was mended, he was back
at *We Care* consoling
a young widow. *Commitment
Phobe*, my friend says when

we see him at a foreign film
with his new rehabilitation
project.  *She looks just like you.*

# On the Crazy Express

you say yes when you mean no
and vice versa as the train
travels down the tracks.

You light brandy on fire
and put it out with a frozen
Daiquiri at the dinner table.

You talk of forever and never
in the same sentence
as the train pulls into the station.

You rewrite history where you
are the victim and I the villain
as we unload baggage and part ways.

I step aboard the Ship of Sanity
but at sea, you show up
with Pinot Noir and Oleander.

and try to woo me into your web.
I get off at the next port
before it sails to Insanity Island.

# Do You Ever Think of Me?

You with all your pedigrees:
MFA, PHD, professor, novelist,
husband and father of five.

Me: the girl in glasses gooey
eyed over your prose
published in the New Yorker

while MS magazine rejects
pathetic pieces I scribble
on toilet paper in the bathroom

of the bars in Mexico
where we sit on stools
bloody red as the bulls

and your face after downing
tequila straight from the bottle,
pickling the worm and you.

Me: the crying fool
who leaves you standing
on the train tracks weaving

and waving before you stumble
back to the suburbs. I picture
you on skid row or in a cemetery,

not on Google. Your dark curly
hair is gone, but I see you and me
in your novels and know the answer.

# Some Have It. Some Don't

the bear of a man
I meet
in Codependents
Anonymous explains.

He sniffs the air
with his snout
as he chomps
on his bacon burger.

*A musky scent*
*pours from her pores.*
He points
to wolf woman
with furry

arms and legs
eating a bowl
of chili clear
across the café.

What scent
do I give off?
I ask,
crossing
my legs

shaved
smooth

and scented
with lavender
lotion.

*I am not*
*attracted*
*to you,*
he says
with a smirk.

I breathe
a sigh of relief
as he reeks
of sweat,
garlic and onions.

# I'm the Wife, She Says

Her voice  as smoky
as the saloon where she
sits on a stool downing
a Bacardi Daiquiri

sucking on a lime
and licking salt
off the rim while
I sip a Singapore Sling,

my voice as sweet
and syrupy as a sunset
sinking behind
the Superstitions.

She is trim as Tammy
with a short shag
while I wear Dolly's
blonde wig and breasts,

which is why he slow
dances with me
to George Jones
on the jukebox

and she shares
her sob story
with the bald
bartender

until the kids run
in and grab him
by the pantleg
and her by the hand,

and they squabble
over who is taking
the night shift before
driving off in the SUV

leaving me to hitch
a ride in a pickup
truck with a cowboy
who smells like a skunk.

# Toddler Houdini

*I've had it,* my girlfriend,
a single mother says
as she tosses her toddler
in my arms. *He ran away.*

An angel in blonde curls
with a devilish smile,
I cuddle the child I wish
was mine in my arms.

*He's not even two. Where could
he go?* I ask. The cops found him
in his Pjs wandering the streets
near the café where she waitresses.

*If my ex finds out, I'll lose him.*
I assure her he's safe with me.
At Wal-Mart he hollers
*Daddy* as his feet dangle

in the shopping cart. A tall
blonde man stares at me
as if I am a kidnapper
until I remind him of who I am.

After his father leaves the store,
I reach for a can on the top shelf
and put it in the basket and the baby
has disappeared. As I run up the aisle

searching frantically, the loudspeaker
booms, *Will the mother please come
pick up her lost blond toddler*. He reaches
out his arms to me and off we go.

As he runs to his mother with an orange
popsicle moustache, she asks me
if he was any trouble. *We had lots
of fun* I say. My little parrot chirps: *Fun*.

# Riding in the Posse

I remember the sun polishing
the brass as the band marched
up the street in the July 4th parade.

Our kids, Ben blowing the bassoon,
Mathew making the saxophone
sing and James pounding the drums.

Firecrackers popping and Rascal,
the Arabian my husband was riding
rearing and him tumbling

backwards, catching his boots
in the stirrups and hanging over
the saddle, until a posse member

grabs the reins and uprights him.
At his father's funeral, we learn
years later that rider was decapitated,

orphaning eight kids, when he spurred
his sorrel who tossed him like a toy
and my husband wasn't there to save him.

# Hide Black Cats On Halloween, the Vets Warn

The myths and tales
of black cats
being scalped
by Satan Worshipers
and boiled in cauldrons
by wicked witches
don't worry my coal
colored frisky felines.
Big Foot, the Bombay,
picks the locks
and prowls
the neighborhood
like a burglar,
feet following
in the footsteps
of masked midgets.
Smoky, the Siamese.
slinks and sneaks
through the open
door as we hand
out sweets
and disappears
into the darkness
returning in the morning
hungry and haughty.
Bella, the Burmese,
arches her back
and fluffs up her tail

as she poses in the window
like a model at Macy's
daring the devils and witches
staring through the glass
to harm a hair on her head.

# The Scottish Country Rock Band

Summer Saturdays, the sound
of bagpipes, harmonica
and acoustical guitar drift
through the open window
of the small apartment
above the bookstore
in Idaho Falls, Idaho
and the elderly neighbors
grab their cane and walkers
and listen from their porches.

As the musicians march down
the stairs and up the sidewalk,
the bookstore customers
pay for their sacks of books
and race out the door. Families
at the garage sale on the corner
buying clothing and collectibles
join in on the clapping.

Cars stop and dogs bark
at the red haired ruddy faced
farm boy in plaid kilts and black
boots blowing the bagpipes,
the Vietnam Vet wearing
his Army fatigues
playing the harmonica
and my husband in jeans
and cowboy hat strumming
his acoustical guitar.

# In the Teepee With the Toddler

*Gramama!* The hazel-eyed toddler
with brown bangs, stares and sheds
his red hoodie and green boots
and grabs Grandpa's walking stick
and props up pillows and blankets
in the bed where I lie on a heating
pad. *Smores*, he shouts and races
to the pantry in the kitchen,
returning with a Hershey bar
and bag of Kraft jumbo mallows.
He climbs into the teepee
and sitting cross-legged
pow wows like an Indian chief.
*What are you doing?*
His father sticks his head in.
*Camping with Gramama,*
he says, face smeared
with marshmallows
and chocolate.

# My Singing Cowboy

*Mama don't let your babies*
*grow up to be cowboys,*
my husband sings Saturdays
channeling Willie and Waylon
as he plucks his electric guitar,
in his black hat and boots
and silver hair at the café,

yogurt shop, laundromat
and the nursing homes
where he plays after Rascal
Sundance, Targhee and Sparky
and the Holstein cows are gone.
.

Cowboying coursed through
his blood, had been handed
down through the generations
as his ancestors rode horses,
herded cattle, slopped pigs,
sheared sheep, delivered lambs,
fished for trout in the rivers,

shot bucks and birds to put food
on the table, living off the land
but in his senior years,
he enjoys the lazy life, singing
songs and watching sunsets
sinking over the Superstitions
satisfying as a strawberry sundae
on a summer Sunday afternoon.

# Poetry Reading at the Bucking Horse Bar on Rodeo Drive

Swiveling on stools,
couples in shorts
chug Cabernet and Coors
as they listen to country music.

My husband plays bass
and Bobby wails Willie
and Waylon, as I sit
at my book table.

On the break, I read poems
from, *My Grandmother Smokes
Chesterfields,* and customers
hand over $20 bills.

The bar owner bans me
from reading poetry
when the band
demands more money

since their tips shrink
when I start selling books.
So during the break,
I read my poems

on the street corner
and sell books
out of the back
of our camper.

# The Color, Cut and Curl

*You should get a beauty*
*license,* my cousin laughs
as she thumbs through
my husband's licenses
to sell insurance, real
estate, recreational
vehicles and mobile homes.

*Don't need one,* he says.
*I have a license to use*
*chemicals,* as he mixes
the solutions in Revlon
Colorsilk, shakes them
and squirts the goop
on my roots and rows
he's raked like the grain
he treated on the farm
in the seventies.

Strands gleam gold
instead of silver
after he snips the split ends
*blow dies and curls,*
and we drive to Daisy's Diner
where the white-haired waitress
asks the name of my hair stylist
as she serves us chicken pot pie,
chocolate pudding and Coca Cola.
I say, *Al at the Color, Cut and Curl.*

# Bailing Our Grandson Out of Jail

*Hi Grandpa*, the voice on the speaker
phone says. *I just got out of the hospital.*
*I was in a car wreck last night. It was*
*the pregnant lady's fault but they arrested*
*me. I couldn't blow in the Breathalyzer*
*because I had blood in my mouth.*

Although he mumbles and moans,
I recognize the voice of our oldest grandson,
who works long days to feed his family
of seven in Utah and never drank a drop.

When he says, *I love you both*, my heart
breaks for our sensitive boy who still
sends us love notes in texts and emails.
*I'm in the courthouse. I need bail money*
*or I'll go to jail.* His voice is shrill
and shreds my heart.

*They couldn't get him on a DUI*
*so, they charged him with reckless*
*driving and failure to take a breathalyzer,*
his attorney says. *This young man*
*has a clean record, If he goes*
*to jail, he may lose his job and his family.*

I am glad he has such a caring attorney.
We offer to pay by debit card or PayPal

but he says we need to buy two blue dot
gift cards from Walgreens 30 miles away.

My husband shakes his head. Points
to the extreme heat warning. *His father
and other grandparents are dead. He's
counting on us*, I say. So we fly down
the highway and call the attorney
from the gift cards section.  A woman
wearing a name tag appears.
*You're being scammed,* she says.
*See he hung up. Call your grandson.*

My husband and I stare speechless,
never dreaming that wasn't our grandson
on the line. He dials and our grandson
answers. He sounds like the imposter
but he is speaking clearly.
*Where are you?* I ask. He laughs.
*At work.* I tell him I'm glad he's okay.
*Your grandparents were scammed,*
the Walgreen's woman informs him.
*You're the best grandparents*, he texts.

We drive home feeling foolish
but now we understand
my in-laws weren't senile
but loving grandparents
when they sent money
to scammers to keep our son
out of jail in Mexico
when he was safe in West Virginia.

# What Forever Feels Like

Alan is an English professor
who dances like John Travolta.
I think he may be the one
until I question him. His jaw hardens.
He leaves me on the dance floor,
and jitterbugs with groupies
who worship him like Ghandi.

Jeff owns a Martial Arts studio,
teaches me Karate and Tai Chi,
serves me salmon salad drizzled
with olive oil for supper. Brings
hot Echinacea tea with a slice
of lemon when I have a cold.
Complains I am neglecting him
because  I am caregiver
for my cancer stricken mother.

Then you show up at my bookstore
fresh from playing racquetball
and running your own real estate
business and we laugh as we learn
to dance and date after divorce.
You make pancakes for my mother
on Sunday mornings and watch
reruns of Dallas with us
and you're still here through
all those decades of love and loss
and taking care of me after my legs
collapse and I can no longer dance.

# Wild Wild West

# Connections

Michael is missing, his mother tells me
as she buys Louis Lamour novels
in my Idaho Falls used bookstore
while the sky is streaked with black clouds.

Although we lived in the same small
town briefly and were the same age,
Michael and I never met but his mother
was a longtime friend of my father's.

Michael's hound howls from her Jeep
Cherokee. The dog was discovered
on the road between Blackfoot
and Pocatello where we drive often.

Her son was last seen with two strangers
in a bar across from the bus station
where my grandmother met the Greyhound
carrying me as a child to Idaho from Montana.

A month later, cops arrest two cowboys
driving Michael's Ford Explorer
with blood in the trunk in Billings
where I was a reporter in the sixties.

His mother won't stop until she finds
her son and puts his murderers in prison.
Michael's body is found near Whitehall
where my father rodeoed in the fifties.

The murderers will die in a prison
near Deet Lodge where we spent the summer.
I understand the grief etched on her
face many years later when I lose my son.

# Cyber Urban Cowboy

He's not John Travolta
and I am not Debra Winger
and we don't fall in love
riding a mechanical bull
in a saloon as Mickey Gilly
sings *lookin' for Love*
in all the wrong places.

He's not Tom Hanks
and I am not Meg Ryan
searching for soul mates
in Seattle and New York City.
Nor are we Robert Redford
and Jane Fonda widowed
and seeking companionship.

He is just an Arizona cowboy poet
and I am a Montana girl who publishes
a poem about cows on the open
Arizona range where I now live.
He leaves a note in the comments
section with his email address.

I email him and get no response
and I google his name looking
for an obit or other tragic news,
and all I see is a photo of a smiling
cowboy in a black hat and shirt
in his bio on Poets & Writers.

I imagine him scribbling poems
around a campfire as he herds
cows up in the mountains,
where there are no cell towers
or Wi-Fi, and when he gets home
he will find my emails piled up
like presents under a tree
and read them over supper
of venison stew and cornbread biscuits.

# Welcome Back to the Old West

The cars are circling the café
like horses at the OK Corral
as we pull our trailer
in front of the Realty Office
to pick up our house key
after nine months in Idaho.


*The scorpion is still in the tub
and the mice had a popcorn
party in your cupboards,*
the blonde woman says.


*Sally and Sam called off the divorce
and aren't selling their ranch,*
she whispers as she hands
us the key. *Collette died of Covid
and Tom bought another mule.*


We see Sally walking on the road
her gray ponytail waving. *Just
getting home?* she asks smiling.
Tom comes galloping up on his mule,
his bald head shiny as the sun.


*Watch out for your new neighbor,*
says the cattle rancher as he points
to a guy in camouflage patrolling
the hill behind our house with a rifle.

*He's a convicted felon on parole.*
*Shot his neighbor and assaulted*
*the deputy who detained him.*
*Don't know how he got out.*

*Welcome Home,* the new neighbor
shouts as the shot rings out
and a quail drops dead at our feet.

# Gunshots Ring Out

I think my husband
is watching reruns
of Gunsmoke on TV.
But the office is empty.

*I hear pop, pop, pop*
as I open the door
and my husband shows up
after dodging bullets on the roof

and grabs an orange vest
and a camera and creeps past cactus,
snapping photos of the utility
truck parked in our driveway

and the man in camouflage
firing bullets from a rifle in one hand,
pistol in the other, as he leans
against a No Shooting Sign.

Fish and Game arrest the shooter
as he drives home in the truck
emblazoned with his name
and cell phone number

after my husband faxes
them the photographs.
The judge gives the shooter
a year in jail and a $1,000 fine.

But that is no consolation
to the mate of the missing
coyote who got a death sentence
for drinking water at our pond.

We mourn with her as we listen
to her howling her heart
out as she stands vigil
over the body night after night.

# Ballad of Big Bad Bob

The General Motors
retired engineer
waddles like a whale
through the Wal-Mart
parking lot to buy raw beef
for the tawny mountain lion
that lives in his driveway
under his copper colored
Lincoln Continental convertible,

smooth and sophisticated
as the Scotch he sips
over ice with his fifth
wife, a skinny blonde
half his age, who drinks
Champagne like water,
and his guests on his patio
when hunters hike the hill
on the side of the golf course
and bullets fly like quail.

*Hold your fire*, he hollers
but when the patio is peppered
with swear words and more bullets
he stomps in the house, grabs his shotgun
and shoots at the hunters who scatter
like leaves in the wind. The cougar
is still crouched under his car, hunters
still shooting, and his wife drinking

champagne on the deck with guests
when he slips in the swimming pool
while sipping scotch and strokes out
on his eighty-ninth birthday.

# Octogenarian Cowboy

Shouts and bellows send
us to the front window
where three gray haired
cowboys in hats hunch
over horses as cattle
huddle in our yard.

When he sees movement
in the window, the craggy
cowboy in charge tips his hat
and I recognize Manny,
and his ranch hands. Two
blue heelers get a drink
out of our pond after
the herd has its fill.

Manny in the lead,
the cowboys herd the cattle
three miles down the dirt
road to Queen Valley
where they vaccinate
and brand the calves
and herd the babies
and mamas back to the desert.

Cars are stopped
on the paved
road from Highway 60
to Queen Valley as a bull

and cows with calves weave
in and out of traffic
and behind them are three
craggy cowboys herding
the cattle off the highway.

On his 90th birthday, a leather
faced bowlegged Manny
ties his horse to an Ironwood
tree and tells us he's sold the ranch.
We still see the old bull
and a few cows and calves
now and then but we miss
the cowboys rounding up
the cattle on Saturday mornings.

# The Cousins were Cowboys

It came natural having trained
on their fathers' farms as children
chasing chickens, gathering eggs,
milking cows, driving tractors.

Then riding horses, corralling cattle,
on their own farms miles apart
in Idaho until they meet again
in the same small town in Arizona.

Now my husband hardly recognizes
Brent with his bloated body and hair
white as the snow on his Idaho farm
as he stands on our step in Arizona.

The last time we saw him he was thin
as a twig, his shaved head sporting
a scar from a surgeon's scalpel
that scooped out a spud sized tumor.

As Brent  bent down to kiss the cold
cheek of his aunt, my husband's mother,
as she lay in her casket, Veronica,
his fit and he althy sister, held him up.

He has come to tell us Veronica
is dead at eighty, three weeks
after a cancer diagnosis. The two
cousins now in their late seventies

hang on to each other as they grieve
like they did when each buried a parent
and brothers many years ago knowing
this may be the last time they meet.

# The Meeting of Champions

July 23, 2012 Mesquite Nevada

My husband recognizes the fit
man in his fifties who passes
us in the parking lot as we head
for Virgin River hotel rooms
although the two cousins
haven't seen each other
in two decades. *Terry?*
my husband asks. *Albert?*

Over prime rib and cheesecake,
Terry asks my husband, *Remember*
*the look on the quarterback's*
*face when you snatched the ball*
*right from under his nose and ran*
*like a rabbit to win the game?*
My husband nods. *Too bad I broke*
*my leg and was benched senior year.*

My husband recalls Terry's college days.
*I remember you slamming wrestler*
*after wrestler to the mat like you did*
*those calves on Grandpa's ranch*
*and winning the national championship*
*even though you were small like me.*
Both were wiry like grandpa, they agreed.

As we soak in the hot tub,
they notice muscles still ripple
under their taller bigger bodies.
*You still doing any wrestling?*
my husband asks Terry.
*Only with sons and grandsons,*
he says, *who want to best the champ.*
*I can still hold my own.* He laughs.

March 28, 2023 Ft. Thomas, AZ

While we are still sleeping seventy
miles away. Terry, now sixty-eight,
is driving his Nissan Ultima
on Highway 70 when a semi going
65 miles per hour swerves
into his lane and hits his car head-on,
slicing it in two and slamming him
against the seat until his spirit sails.
Forty tons of steel has taken out the champ.

# Our Grandchildren's Other Grandfather

His scuffed Stetsons
sit by his stirrups
and saddle in the shop.

His cowboy hat hangs
with his fringed jacket
on the rack in the hall.

Shriveled to a sliver
of himself, he lies
in the hospice bed

in the same room
in the farmhouse
where he was born.

The dead - his wife
 and two sons- watch
from photographs

as friends and family
file in. He opens milky
eyes and smiles as he stares

into the wide blue pupils –
identical to his as a boy -.
of his and our infant great

granddaughter as her mother,
his and our granddaughter,
kisses his leathery cheek

and our daughter, who sees
him as a second father,
pats his gnarly hand.

Our and his other grandchildren
sponge his parched lips while
the nurse administers morphine.

When he takes his last breath
three months from his 80th birthday
the wind howls through the pasture.

# Tanya Tucker Wannabe

You stand barefoot
on the stage
in faded jeans
and curly red hair
strumming the guitar
Grandpa bought you
as you growl: *Delta Dawn*
*What's that flower*
*You Got On* at thirteen
the same age as Tanya
when she hit Number 1.
Applause says star power.
Thirteen years later
do you ever pick up
the guitar and strum
and sing as you cuddle
your cowboy, children
and canines in the suburbs?

# Mustang Mama

For many moons, she rocks
her little one to sleep
in her womb

as the wind whistles
and the sparrows sing,
her wide hips swinging

and sashaying as the stallion
leads and she and his eight
other sister wives follow

on the dance floor
of the Salt River Basin,
their manes wet and wild,

then showering, swimming
and paddling up to their necks,
dining on greens, sunflowers

and fresh sodium water
and when the foal drops
between her legs,

her filly or colt will salsa
and swim with the wild horses
as the scarlet sun rises and sets.

# Where There's Smoke

I am sleeping in on Saturday morning
when the phone rings, but by the time
I answer it, the caller has hung up.

I go back to bed, and am awakened
by a frantic banging on the back door
so I pull on my robe and head for the kitchen.

The caretaker at the old homestead
northeast of us by a quarter of a mile
is already pulling away in his jeep

which looks like Noah's Ark
with a Doberman in front, a Boxer
in back and six cats in crates.

But it is what I see in the background
which has me panicking. Helicopters
dumping buckets of water on flames

shooting high in a smoky sky
with only a grassy hill and road
between our house and the fire

and my husband is thirty miles
away with our only car
jamming with musicians

in Cobb's Café in Apache Junction.
*There's a fire on the other side
of the hill,* I shriek into the cell.

Alarm bells ring in his ears. *On my way,*
he says and I hear the tires rolling on the freeway.
I am packed and watching helicopters

dumping buckets of water but the flames
rage on when my husband pulls into
the garage and informs me the fire

is actually three miles away burning
down the Eucalyptus and Cottonwood
trees behind the dam where we picnicked

with the grandkids in our "Secret Place,
where we found shade and tree branches
strong enough to sit in and swing. *The trees*

*are falling into the fire and the whole
forest is already blackened,* my husband
says as my stomach sinks. *We aren't in danger,*

he says the fireman told him unless the wind
changes direction. The fire is extinguished
by nighttime but the secret was out.

The deadly enemy had invaded our space
and destroyed our secret spot
where we sneaked away for shade

as the temperatures soared into the triple
digits. That was over sixteen years ago
and the greenery grew back quickly

but although our secret place is right
behind the mailboxes, we've never
returned because it's not special anymore.

# Standoff at Elephant Butte

A middle-aged Cinderella
in a cowgirl hat and boots
and chickens in cages

squawking from the backseat
of her SUV pulling mustangs
in a horse trailer, Cassandra

rides onto the desert land
ruled by cows and coyotes
for centuries and her first order

of business is to get rid
of the cows and coyotes,
she announces to us,

who have lived in a house
with a waterfalls and pond
at Elephant Butte for two decades.

*Cowpies are unsanitary.*
*Coyotes will kill my chickens,*
she tells my husband

as she demands he shut
down our pond watering
wildlife and range cows.

No watering deer, birds,

Etc. No animals you don't
*own,* the Fraulein Hitler

declares in the cease and desist
order she nails on our door
and when we don't comply

she pounds on our doors
*and windows and peaks*
through our blinds.

My husband sends Cassandra
a letter by certified mail
accusing her of trespassing

and harassment. *We'll sue,*
he threatens if she doesn't get
her horse trailer and corral

off our property line. A blue
shed and five attack dogs
straining on chains

appear on the property line
and as she sits on the fence
we wait inside barricaded

behind clay walls for the first
shot to be fired like Randy
Weaver at Ruby Ridge.

# The Chicken Dance

Rudy the red rooster
toots his trumpet
to wake us at dawn
and at noon leads
his ten hefty hens
across our green lawn,
feathers fluffing and flouncing,
beaks cackling and clucking
toes two stepping and tapping
to the rhythmic snoring
of the feral feline
full of Fancy Feast
snoozing on the sofa
in our sun porch
while we watch
through the window
as we lunch on tuna salad
sandwiches and iced tea.

# Canine Rock Band

We hear distinctive voices
like the Rolling Stones
from a pack of dogs
on a nearby parcel.

The lead singer in the band,
an English Bull Dog tethered
to the horse trailer growls
and gyrates like Jagger.

The German Shepherd,
secured to the shed,
whines and wails
like Richards' lead guitar.

A basset hound chained
to an Ironwood barks
in a deep low tone
like Wyman's bass guitar.

The booming voice
of the Golden Retriever
roped to the RV
is loud as Watts drums.

The Siberian Huskey
hitched to the horse trailer
howls like the harmonica
played by Jones.

As we listen to the concert,
my husband remembers
two dogs attacking him
on his paper route.

Shows me the half moon
scar on his right calf
where a Collie tore flesh
when he was eight.

And he breathes hard
like he did at eleven
after a heavy hound
knocks him down
and sits on his chest
chewing through the bag
of newspapers protecting him
until the owner pulls it off

*I was afraid of dogs for a long
time,* he says, but now I watch
as he walks past the barking,
snarling pack of dogs

while I stay inside, sweating
like in my sleep seven decades
after two large Labradors
run out into the street snarling,

knocking me down, ripping
my clothes as I walk to school
day after day, year after year
and no one ever rescues me.

# Nature's Designer Cat

The face of a fox swivels
over the spotted shoulder
of a bodacious bobcat body,

while the long tail of a tiger
tabby twitches as our guest
savors the smorgasbord

in the sunlight from our yard
in the Arizona desert
where a pack of coyotes

stalk and snatch squirrels
and small pets for snacks
under the cover of darkness.

This cat picks the chicken
carcass clean, bypassing
banana and cucumber peels,

before sharpening
its claws on the bark
of an Ironwood tree

and with the confidence
of a cougar strutting
on a catwalk, disappears

behind Mesquite bushes
Cholla and Saguaro
into the Arizona desert.

# Feathers and Fur Fly

at the cat dish
in the sunporch
sometime between
dusk and dawn

as we sleep
soundly
on the other side
of the glass.

Since the cat is silent
as we sweep up
the wings, tail
and feathers

and doesn't devour
the turkey meatball
we deposit
in his dish,

we speculate
the cactus
wren flies
in the courtyard,

smells salmon
and slips
through the slit
in the screen

not seeing
the tabby
sleeping
on the scaffold

and is surprised
when ambushed
as it scarfs
down the Meow Mix..

# March Usually Rides in on a Bucking Bronc

with her long red hair
tangled and teased
by a wild wind.

But this year, she strolls
in astride a white stallion
her hair stuffed in a stocking

cap and hands in mittens
tossing snow like confetti
on the mountain tops

and spreading a white blanket
over the green grass on our lawn
to protect it from the frost

so that when the sun shines
the greenery will smile
and sparkle and look forward

to spring dancing in the desert
with fists full of flowers
like a barefoot bride.

# Red Headed Stranger

I hear repeated knocks
on the kitchen door
as I am eating
my burger, fries
and corn on the cob.

I freeze and wait
for the person to appear
in the front yard, peering
through the window
because I don't open
my door to strangers.

Instead, I see a head
playing peek a boo
around the pine pole
on the porch
like an annoying
first grader
on the playground

and recognize
the pileated woodpecker
with his thatch of red
hair and beak nose
and don't let him in
no matter how long
or loud he knocks.

# Growing Old in the West

### *Your Blood must be Sweet,* **he says**

after putting a flame
to the back of my knee
coaxing a brown tick
from its burrow beneath
my skin where it feasts

on the smorgasbord
of my blood as we hike
in Beaverhead-Deer Lodge
National Forest in Montana
when I am seventeen.

More than seven decades
later, I am kickboxing
in my Arizona home
near Tonto National Forest
when my right foot itches
near the base of my middle toe.

As I scratch my skin,
my nails unearth a mound
and a tick marches out.
*Your blood must still be sweet,*
he says and I smile.

# Father's Day June 19, 1989

I try to hide my irritation when
my father greets me at the door
wearing the blue shirt and slacks
my sister sent from San Francisco
instead of waiting for me to arrive
before opening the package.

He's 81, and in his second childhood,
my mother, who was six years younger
would remind me, but my father
never grew up. Before it was time
to open our Christmas presents,

he'd play the game, *What's in the Box?*
Pick up one of our presents and say,
*I think it's a doll,* spoiling the surprise
and try to convince us to tell him
what we got him for Christmas.

Always the practical child, I hand
him my unwrapped presents
tied with a bow: a carton of Camels,
a box of chocolates and a bottle
of Tylenol to ease his headaches.

If I could replay that day, I wouldn't
have just given him gifts and left.
I would have instead hugged him,
kissed his cheek, told him I loved

him and that he was a good father
and asked him to forgive me
for being suspicious and ashamed of him
when I smelled whiskey on his breath.

But even if I knew then what I know now-
that would be his last Father's Day -
I couldn't say those words *I love you*
and *forgive me* because he never said
that to me but I always knew and he did too.

# Heir to the Throne

Just as my father is getting ready
to check out of Hotel Earth,
my nephew swims through my sister's
birth canal and when the two sets
of piercing black eyes and bald heads

meet they smile as if gazing
into a mirror. When my father takes
a bow and exits the stage,
his grandson takes up his passion
for cooking and reading and writing.

I see my father's smiling eyes
and hear his laughter as I watch
my nephew receive his diploma
in English and recite the works
of Steinbeck, Hemingway and Poe

to a classroom full of students
who find him humorous and brilliant
and writing short stories in his office
while his wife and children sleep
just like his grandfather, my father.

And now on my nephew's 39th birthday
I watch my father 's tall slim body bend
over the backyard grill as his grandson
flips sirloin steaks in the sunlight
and serves them on paper plates

with the grace of his grandfather
who is somewhere grilling steaks
and teaching grammar content
his grandson is carrying on
in the kingdom he built for him.

# Thanksgiving With the In Laws

*Dad, won't you let me drive*, my husband
says. But my 94-year-old father-in-law
waves his driver's license in his son's face
and wobbles on his cane to his 2006 Buick
LeSabre and sits in the driver's seat
like a king on a throne. The Buick backs out

of the driveway and we creep
down the highway like a caterpillar
while all the cars and trucks pass us –
my husband in the front passenger
seat and my mother-in-law and me
in the back seat - pretending not to notice.

He waits at the wheel while we walk
into Wal-Mart and buy a turkey, yams,
Stovetop dressing, Jello, fruit cocktail
and cranberry sauce. His hand shakes
as he slices the turkey meat in slivers
but when his knees buckle he lets
my husband carve and carry the turkey

to the table. He laughs and smiles
as his grandkids and great grandkids
show up from Utah and Washington
and pile turkey, stuffing, mashed
potatoes soft as snow on the ground,
gravy, marshmallow roasted yams
and pumpkin pie on their plates.

He naps in his recliner as the grandkids
romp in the pasture and barn
where he sheered the sheep and helped
the ewes deliver their lambs. I can still
see him standing on the step waving
as we drive back to our homes, none
of us knowing the stroke will strike
like a tornado the next summer
and this will be our last Thanksgiving
as a family with our patriarch.

# Larry and Gerry Gene

Closer than cousins,
better than big brothers,
Larry, Gerry Gene and I
ride through our childhood
Larry as Roy Rogers,
Gerry as Gene Autry
and me as Dale Evans,
with our dogs, Smoky, Pepper,
and Tootsie trotting behind.

After high school Larry joins
the Army and Gerry gets
married and I move
to Billings to work
on the Gazette. In a Billings
Bar, Gerry, his wife, my sister
and I drink foaming beer
in mugs as the country
crooner sings cheating songs.

A big man grabs me with muscular
arms and pulls me on his lap,
and as he rubs his red beard against
my face and tries to kiss my cheek,
I struggle to get away. *Let go of me,*
I protest. Gerry and the others laugh.

*Don't you recognize  me, Cuz?*
the stranger says in Larry's

voice. I laugh and hug him tight.
*When did you get home?*
I ask. Now Gerry is gone, leaving
Larry and me to connect on computers
with the help of our grandchildren.

# Frankie and Dave

Frankie's boss at the bakery
tells him his sister came
to take him to lunch.
*I don't have a sister,* he says.
*She looks just like you.
Blonde. Dimples*
.

He knows right away
it is me. In my twenties
I never dream he will die
by the age of forty-five.

His brother Dave calls from Mesa
where he recently moved.
1 am seventy and he sixty.  A man
with my grandfather's face
walks right up to me and hugs me.

At The Flying Monkey Saloon,
Dave sits beside me drinking
a Bud draft. One by one,
senior single women
suddenly slide in the booth
smiling. *Introduce me
to your brother*, they say.

# Crow's Feet

Through the bedroom
window glass I watch
wrinkled feet with onyx
painted toenails two step
across the sill, hear cawing
and a flutter off wings
and blink at a black blur.
As I sleep, I dream Mr. Crow
is tap dancing across the floor
of my face like Fred Astaire
barefoot in black coattails
and in the morning
I look in the mirror and find
the proof – his footprints
in the corner of each eye.

# Surprise, My Husband Says

as he stands in the doorway
while I hunch over the computer.
*Guess what I found in the garage?*
*A rattlesnake*, I answer.
He laughs and I keep typing.
*Can't this wait until I finish my poem?*

*No.* He whirls my chair around,
takes my hand and kneels down.
*Close your eyes*, he says, and I feel
something sliding on my finger.
*Now you can open your eyes*, he says.

Winking at me like a sparkling star
is my missing solitaire diamond ring
I picked out after he proposed
and the gold band that sealed
the deal in the hot air balloon
floating over Reno many moons ago.

I never take it off, even when
I fall while doing the tree pose
and break all my fingers
and they swell like sausages
and the ring tightens like a vice
cutting off my circulation.

When the swelling shrinks
and the ring slips and slides

like a seal on a sandy beach,
I just wrap tape around it.
Then one day five years ago
as I put avocados in the bin
I notice my ring finger is naked.

We empty drawers like burglars,
retrace our steps and query
clerks at Wal-Mart, the Dollar
Store, Superstition Market
but they all shake their heads.
We check the parking lots,
storm drains, pawn shops,
eBay, make a police report,
Even glance at ring fingers
of friends and strangers.

We can't bring ourselves
to replace it. *I have a feeling
we will find it someday,* I say
but my hope fades as the years
come and go. Still the solitaire
sits near the water tank waiting
as we walk by for us to look down
and pick it up and put it back
on my finger where it belongs.

# The Great Grand Moments

of our life are memorialized
on our wall. Our youngest
grandson at two sits on the stool
of the grand piano of his great
grandmother and his teenage
brother, solemnly stares at sea,
while his father steers the boat,
as his girlfriend, wrapped
in a wool blanket, sleeps head
on his shoulder. Their grandfather
smiles from a sofa surrounded by six
great grandchildren from twos
to teens. Our youngest great
grandchild, tiny as a teacup
blue eyes big as saucers
balances on her mother's palm
like her mother teetered
on the rim of the Grand Canyon
at twelve with her cousin,
both now twenty-four. Two
other teen grandsons play
guitars like their father
before them and the circle
of life spins round and round.

# On Father's Day 2023

Our fourth great grandson
and eighth great grandbaby
shows up in a Vancouver
delivery room at 2 am
sporting a full head
of dark hair, weighing
eight pounds and measuring
twenty three inches just like
our son and grandson
when they were born.

His father and grandfather
stretch their six foot three
bodies and long lanky legs
while his great-grandfather
sleeps soundly in Phoenix.
The baby wears the same
round pug nosed face
as his paternal grandmother
who cradles him as he snoozes.

# On Our Son's Facebook Page

We find no photos of him,
no mention of places
where he lived
except for the town
where he grew up.

No mention of us, his siblings,
fellow sailors or several pets.
Only two photos of his sons
as children and teenagers
swinging in hammocks

And posts on fundraisers
he organized for St. Jude's,
The Wounded Warrior's Project,
and Wildcat Sanctuary.

On Facebook, he has
no friends when in life
his friends are many.

He isn't accepting friend
requests and hasn't posted
since he donated  money

to the Sea Turtle Conservancy.
for the birthday of the mother
of his two sons because
13 days later his life ended.

# On the Second Anniversary of His Death

His white and blue hat
sailors salute on the submarine
sits on the glass hutch
beside the empty urn.

In the windowsill,
a spider on stilts
spins a web that snares
a buzzing bumblebee.

Outside, a Sonoran toad
weeps and wails as rain
washes him from his
underground bunker.

When the sun smiles,
baby bald eagles
chirp from their nest
in the Saguaro Cactus.

# Splashing in Sunlight

Like a goldfish, she swims
into my dream, her arms
paddling, her breath
gulping fresh air before
she is swallowed by space.

My husband and I question
her silent, smiling mother.
I accuse her of the unthinkable.
She says: *I saw this house.*
*I left her there. I thought you knew.*

I follow her down the road
to the white house.
Hope in my heart, I gaze
through glass and all I see
is dust covered furniture.

I hear the little girl breathing,
singing, laughing, watch her
dancing among the dandelions,
splashing in sunlight
until she swims out of sight.

# Mothers of Lost Children

Whether they disappear
at birth, childhood
or adulthood,
yesterday
or a century ago,
we still swim
in a Sea of Sadness,
seeing their reflection
in the water,
waving our arms
as rescue boats float by.
Once onshore, we return
to our lives, until memories
wash over us like waves
and the tide threatens to pull us
under and that's when hope
steps in and saves us from sinking.

# Weeping Birch

Silver and bent,
she's weeping again
outside the window.
Tanned slender arms
drooping in despair
and sorrow. Shedding
tears on the lawn
as she rocks
bawling baby
robins. Mourning
her lost loved ones?
Or can she hear
me sobbing
through the glass
as I write
the obituaries
of my son
and mother-in-law.
Is she still weeping
or did the developers
put her out
of her misery?

# Tangles

*Maybe I should shave my head*,
I say as strands of hair float
in the air like spider webs.

Or cut it short as yours,
as it skims soup and tickles
my thigh as I type.

*You would not be you*
*without long hair,* he says
as he hands me the brush.

*What about my tangles?*
He is speechless as I sit
on the side of the bed

expecting a baby wren
to fly from the nest
matted on the back

of my head but the brush
smooths eight decades
of tangles in my life

and love and we lie
side by side and sleep
soundly in the silence.

# I Call My Daughter After We Put the Turkey in the Oven

*Happy Thanksgiving.*
She gasps for air and I know
she's having a panic attack.

*What's wrong?* I ask,
not wanting to know.
*I have bad news.*

I imagine a grandchild
or great grandchild blue
and cold in a morgue.

Now I am gasping. *Tell me.*
She says our oldest grandson fell
fifteen fee but *he's alive.*

I breathe better until she says:
*Spinal cord injury.*  I smother a sob
as I tell his grandfather.

My husband texts his grandson
whom he thinks of as a son
in the hospital: *So Sorry.*

*We are praying for you*
and he answers instantly.
*Thank you. I love you.*

We sigh in relief hoping
that means no brain trauma,
remembering our panic

when our oldest son fell thirty feet
imagining internal and head injuries
and he survived with broken bones.

As we eat cranberry sauce
and pumpkin pie, we picture
our grandson in a hospital bed

eating turkey and trimmings
on a tray as his six-year-old
daughter wipes gravy from his chin.

# Care Loving

He brings her strawberries
and cream from the market
since the garden has gone
to weeds and the cow dried up.

Spoon feeds her as she sits
on the edge of the bed,
her silver hair streaming
over her nightgown.

Lifts her light body, lowers
her in the warm water
and washes her dry skin
with moisturizing body wash.

After she falls asleep,
he remembers soaking
in the tub and waltzing
skin to skin before the stroke.

He hears her moan and asks
if she's okay and she smiles.
He wonders if she is having
the same memories.

# Staying Alive

My father was pushing
82 -  the same age
as I am now - when
he went to sleep and never
woke up. When I succumb
to sleep in the darkness
I am surprised when the sun
shines and birds sing.

It is pitch black and I awaken
to the crowing of the rooster
and know he is communicating
with his hens like he does
in the daytime when they stroll
across our property.

I hope the chickens are in the coop
and the feral cat is curled up
on the couch in the sunporch
because I hear the yipping
of a pack of coyotes hoping
for raw meat for breakfast.

I close my eyes again and sunlight
splashes me awake. The chickens
are cackling and pecking
and the tabby Is standing
outside the door waiting
for his breakfast and unlike my father
I have lived to see another day.

# What To Do With My Body After I Die

*Cremation is cheaper*, my husband says.
But the voice of the Pentecostal preacher
still echoes in my head, *You'll burn
in hell for your sins*. Why did I give up
clandestine rendezvous, Kalua & cream,
and filet mignon to burn my body
until it turns to dust like the dirt
I vacuumed up for years
when I had more fun sinning?

The undertaker shows me stainless
steel boxes that keep bodies
preserved like pickled pigs feet
but my claustrophobia kicks
in and I reach for my inhaler. *Donate
your body to science*, the sign
says, but I cannot picture students
the age of my grandchildren gawking
at my skeleton and pointing out
my imperfections., *Sleep on it*, my sister says.

*Always wear clean underpants
in case you get in an accident*,
my mother taught me
before we buried her in a pine box
more than two decades ago
so I put on Tide scented bikini panties
before I slip between the sheets just in case
one of the fighter jets careening
overhead crashes and burns on our roof.

# About the Author

Pushcart Prize and Best of the Net Nominated Poet Sharon Waller Knutson is a retired journalist who lives in Arizona. She has published twelve poetry books including *My Grandmother Smokes Chesterfields* (Flutter Press 2014,) *What the Clairvoyant Doesn't Say* and *Trials & Tribulations of Sports Bob* (Kelsay Books 2021) and *Survivors, Saints and Sinners* (Cyberwit 2022,) *Kiddos & Mamas Do the Darndest Things* (Cyberwit 2022,) *The Vultures are Circling* (Cyberwit 2023) and *The Leading Ladies in My Life* (Cyberwit June 2023.) .Her work has also appeared in *Poetry Breakfast, Autumn Sky Poetry Review, Poetry Hunger X, Lothlorien, GAS Poetry, Art and Music, The Rye Whiskey Review, Black Coffee Review, ONE ART, Mad Swirl, The Drabble, Gleam, Muddy River Review, Verse-Virtual, Your Daily Poem, Red Eft Review, Beatnik Cowboy, The Five-Two, Impspired and others.*